HUMPBACK WHALES

Dorothy Hinshaw Patent

photographs by

Deborah A. Glockner-Ferrari
and Mark J. Ferrari

Holiday House/New York

All photographs were taken under federal permit
granted by the National Marine Fisheries Service
and state permit granted by the State of Hawaii
Department of Land and Natural Resources.
D.A.G.-F. and M.J.F.

Library of Congress Cataloging-in-Publication Data
Patent, Dorothy Hinshaw.
Humpback whales / written by Dorothy Hinshaw Patent ; illustrated
with full color photos by Mark J. Ferrari and Deborah A. Glockner-Ferrari.
—1st ed.
p.   cm.
Summary: Describes the physical characteristics, habitat, and
behavior of the humpback whale.
ISBN 0-8234-0779-9
1. Humpback whale—Juvenile literature.   [1. Humpback whale.
2. Whales.]   I. Ferrari, Mark J., ill. II. Glockner-Ferrari,
Deborah A., ill. III. Title.
QL737.C424P37   1989
599.5—dc19   89-2026   CIP   AC

For all those who work to save the whales

D.H.P.

To our loving parents, Wilfred and Elrita Glockner
and Harold and Dorothy Ferrari

D.A.G.-F. and M.J.F.

The humpback whale is a very big animal, even when it is a baby. When it's born, the young humpback, called a calf, is already 14 feet long and weighs as much as a large station wagon. By the time it's a year old, it is 30 feet long and weighs twice as much.

Even though it is very big, the humpback is strong enough to get its body out of the water.

An adult humpback whale is huge. It is 62 feet long. That's as long as ten men lying head to foot on the floor. It weighs 53 tons, as much as ten elephants.

Humpbacks are strange-looking animals. Their small eyes are just above the curve of their long mouths. Their throats have many grooves that look like stripes. The grooves allow the throat to get bigger when the whale feeds.

You can see the mouth, eye, and throat grooves on this young humpback.

The humpback has four fins. Two, called flippers, lie on each side of the body, just behind the mouth. Their front edges are wavy, with bumps on them. The flippers are 13 to 15 feet long, longer than those of any other whale.

A third fin sticks up on top of the whale. It sits toward the back of the body and is called the dorsal fin.

The dorsal fin of the whale in front looks like it was once injured.

Each humpback has a different pattern on its flippers and the underside of its flukes.
This is how scientists recognize individual whales.

Then there is a fin at the end of the whale's body. It forms the whale's tail. The two halves of the tail fin are called flukes. The flukes move up and down in the water, pushing the animal forward.

Whales can live a long time. Humpbacks survive for thirty years or more. Barnacles often grow on their bodies. At least three different kinds of barnacles live on different parts of humpback whales.

You can see the barnacles on the face of this humpback.

The whale's eyes may look small. But that's just because the whale is so big. Humpbacks can see quite well both underwater and in the air. The whale can move its eyes so that it can see in different directions.

The whale's ears are completely inside its head. Only a small slit can be seen where the ear opens to the outside. Whales have very good hearing. They make sounds to "talk" to one another. Some of these sounds may carry for many miles through the water.

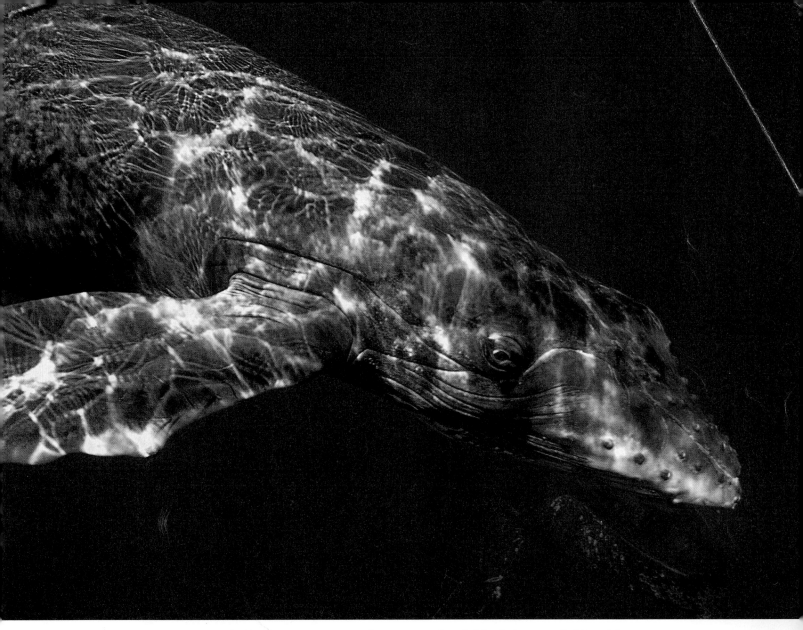

If you look closely, you can see the ear opening behind the eye of this calf.

Touching one another seems to be important to whales. Humpbacks sometimes use their long fins to stroke each other. The whale calf often touches its mother with its body.

This calf is floating along upside down, using its fins to keep its position.

Whales cannot smell, but they probably are able to taste. Their sense of balance is very good. When a humpback is underwater, it looks as if it is floating along. It uses small movements of its side fins and flukes to keep its balance in the water.

Humpbacks have a two-part blowhole.

Whales are mammals, as are dogs and horses. Like all mammals, they breathe air. On the top of the head the whale has a blowhole. It lets air out of the blowhole when it comes to the surface. Then it takes in new air. When the whale breathes out, it makes a spout called a blow.

Humpbacks live in all the world's oceans. They spend the summer near the North Pole and the South Pole, where there is lots of food. In the winter, they travel, or migrate, to warmer waters.

Many humpbacks, like these three, spend the winter in Hawaiian waters.

In North America, humpbacks live along both coasts. The western whales spend the summer in Alaskan waters. Then they swim thousands of miles to live in Hawaii or Mexico during the winter.

A humpback in Alaska.

The largest population of humpbacks lives along the east coast of North America. Many of these whales feed during the summer in Canadian waters or in the Gulf of Maine. Others go all the way to Greenland and Iceland. Then they make a long trip to Puerto Rico and nearby Silver Bank for the winter.

Humpbacks off Newfoundland.

During the summer, humpbacks must eat all the food they need for a year. While in polar waters, they feed on small fish that live in big schools. They also eat tiny shrimplike animals that swarm by the millions.

Humpbacks feed on fish such as these capelin.

The head of this feeding humpback is sideways, and its mouth is wide open. You can see the baleen attached to the upper jaw.

Humpbacks don't have teeth. They have baleen instead, flat bony plates that hang down from the upper jaw in rows. The baleen is tough and flexible. The inner edges of the plates are fringed.

The mouth of this feeding humpback is partly open. You can see the baleen inside.

When the humpback whale feeds, it gulps in big mouthfuls of water. The grooves on its throat expand to make the mouth enormous. Then the whale closes its mouth partway. It pushes the water out through the gaps between the baleen plates. The fringed edges act like strainers so that the fish and other food stay inside the mouth.

Whales store energy in a fat layer underneath the skin called blubber. The blubber is up to 3 to 4 inches thick after a summer of feeding. It is especially thick on the bodies of pregnant female whales. Later, the mother whale must nourish her baby as well as herself for the whole winter with her stored fat.

Under the skin of the humpback is a thick layer of blubber.

After the whales arrive near their warm winter homes, the calves are born. The humpback calf knows how to swim from the moment of its birth. It stays close to its mother. Usually, the baby swims just above its mother's body, almost touching it.

The whale calf feeds on its mother's milk. The milk is very rich. It looks like condensed milk. About 90 percent of cow's milk is water, but only about half of humpback milk is water. The calf nurses from teats tucked away in slits on the mother's belly. The calf nurses many times during the day.

A calf nursing.

Winter is also mating time. Male humpbacks have their own way of getting noticed. They sing long, complex songs with many notes. Some of the notes are high and squeaky. Others are low and rumbly. These songs can be heard miles away. While singing, the whale lies still in the water with its head down.

Male humpbacks fight with each other during the mating season.

A singing humpback.

In one area, all the whales sing the same song each year. But the song changes somewhat from year to year. It seems that only male humpbacks sing. They may be telling other males to stay away. Or they may be trying to attract females.

During the summer, a male whale often swims along with a female and her calf. This whale is called an escort. The escort whale is probably there to mate with the female.

Mating takes place about eleven-and-a-half months before birth. Some female humpbacks have a calf every year. But most bear young every two or three years.

A mother humpback with her calf and an escort. The escort is blowing bubbles.

Today there are about 10,000 humpback whales. That may sound like a lot. But there were once at least 100,000 of them. Humpback whales, like other kinds, used to be hunted for their valuable blubber. Other parts of the whale's body were used too. Now, humpbacks are protected from hunting by international laws. Let's hope these laws keep the humpback whale from dying out.

INDEX
(Italicized numbers indicate photos.)

Alaska, *20*

balance, 17
baleen, *23–24*
barnacles, 12, *13*
blow, 18
blowhole, *18*
blubber, *25*
breathing, 18

calf, 5, *15*, *17*, *26–27*, *30*
   birth, 27
   nursing, *27*
   size, 5
Canada, 21

ears, 14, *15*
escort whale, *30*
eyes, *7*, 14 *15*

feeding, *22–24*
fins, 9, *10*, 11, 16, 17
flippers, *8*, *9*, *11*
flukes, *11*, 17

Greenland, 21
Gulf of Maine, 21

Hawaii, *19*, 20

Iceland, 21

lifespan of humpbacks, 12

male humpbacks, *28–30*
mammals, 18
mating, 28, 30
Mexico, 20
migration, 19–20
milk of humpback, 27
mouth, *7*

Newfoundland, *21*
numbers of humpbacks, 31

Puerto Rico, 21

range of humpbacks, 19–21

Silver Bank, 21
size of humpbacks, 5–6
songs of humpbacks, 28–29
sounds, 14, 28–29

taste, 17
teats, 27
throat grooves, *7*, 24
touch, 16

whaling, 31
weight of humpbacks, 5–6